To

From

Author is represented by Mick Silva Editing, Portland, OR.

Cover and interior design by Jeff Jansen | www.AestheticSoup.net. Cover art: Creative Market/Sammy Arnault-Ham | creativemarket.com

Ellie Claire
Hachette Book Group
1290 Avenue of the Americas, New York, NY 10104
ellieclaire.com

First Edition: February 2019

Ellie Claire is a division of Hachette Book Group, Inc. The Ellie Claire name and logo are trademarks of Hachette Book Group, Inc.

Library of Congress Cataloging-in-Publication Data has been applied for.

ISBN: 978-1-63326-211-9 (hardcover)

Printed in China

RRD

10 9 8 7 6 5 4 3 2 1

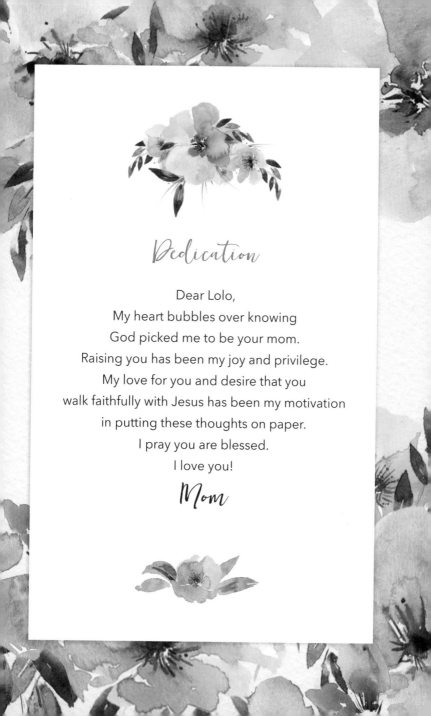

Dedication

Dear Lolo,
My heart bubbles over knowing
God picked me to be your mom.
Raising you has been my joy and privilege.
My love for you and desire that you
walk faithfully with Jesus has been my motivation
in putting these thoughts on paper.
I pray you are blessed.
I love you!

Mom

Note

*Anne Ortlund was a spiritual grandmother
to my daughter and a beloved friend and
mentor to me. Before her death, she wrote a
foreword to this book, that at the time was
solely for my daughter. Her words have
been such a beautiful blessing that I wanted
to share them with all the young women who
will hold this book in their hands. May you
be as blessed by Anne's words as we have.*

Foreword

My Dear Girl,
I'm so honored to write the foreword to this book from
your mother to you. I encourage you to read it over
and over all your life, and if the Lord gives you children,
to pass it on to them too. Your mother is careful to
obey the Scriptures, which includes these words:

*Tell the next generation the praiseworthy
deeds of the Lord...so the next generations
would know them, and even the children
yet to be born, and they in turn would tell
their children. Then they would put their trust
in God and would not forget his deeds
but would keep his commands.*
Psalm 78:4, 6–7 NIV

May God richly bless you and your future
generations until Jesus Christ comes!

I love you.
Anne Ortlund

Introduction

I've always known Jesus is the main thing in life; my sweet grandma told me regularly. I can still hear her voice reminding me of what was most important. She was loving, kind, patient, and humble. Her words and priorities matched up and I took notice. Journeying through life, I've settled here too: Jesus is the main thing!

Putting these thoughts on paper, it's been my goal to pass on the nuggets of wisdom and tips I've discovered that have grounded me in my faith. The wisdom offered here has been hard-fought. I've made plenty of blunders.

*I urge you to live life with God because I often
bulldozed ahead on my own and made
a mess of things. I warn you to beware of pride
because I've struggled there and want you to
avoid the traps I've fallen into. I hope you'll
learn to say no because a busy, chaotic life will
leave you frazzled and unfulfilled. I know this
from experience. Thankfully God's hallmarks are
love and grace and He isn't finished with us yet!*

*Working out my faith in daily submission
has been worth the fight. I've learned
peace comes through surrender, contentment
follows obedience, and preferring others
really does produce joy.*

*I pray this little book inspires you
to live courageously!*

1

Keep Jesus the Main Thing

He is amazing, everlasting God! He is truth and life, love and hope. He is God Almighty and Friend of sinners. In Him you'll discover your true identity as a beloved child of God, and because of Him you are worthy and welcome in God's family. Who could ask for more? Remember, Jesus *is* and will *always be* the Main Thing!

2

Spread Kindness

Kindness reflects the heart of God. Being friendly and gracious by offering a warm smile, a timely word of encouragement, or a thoughtful invitation may give another the strength to keep going on a rough day. True kindness isn't something you can muster up; it is the natural result of the Holy Spirit taking residence in your heart. So be generous with your sweet smile, spreading kindness wherever you go, putting the heart of God on display.

3

Keep Reading

Developing the love of reading will help you become a lifelong learner. Make it your habit to have a book on your bedside table and in your car. When you have unexpected time on your hands, having a book handy means you won't be wasting time and you will be learning and growing.

4

Live Life with God

The promise of God's presence, what a gift! Take Him at His word and learn to enjoy life *with* Him. Living with God means you are never alone; He is your constant companion, teacher, and guide. He knows your thoughts, so turn your internal dialog into a conversation with Him. He cares about your burdens and wants to share your joy. Be attentive and listen for His voice. He has so much to reveal to you. Abundant life with God is yours for the taking; don't settle for less!

The King will reply,
"Truly I tell you,
whatever you did for
one of the least of these
brothers and sisters of mine,
you did for me."

MATHEW 25:40 NIV

5

Look with His Eyes

*I*magine how different the world would be if all were motivated by mercy and compassion. Keep an eye out for people who are hurting; be a friend to someone who needs one. Don't let image management keep you from helping a brother or sister in need; ask God to break your heart over the things that break His. You will join God in important work. Nothing is more fulfilling!

6

Embrace the Gift of Prayer

Prayer is a precious gift to be received, practiced, and enjoyed. Share your heart with God and you will enjoy intimacy with the Creator as you listen, talk, and wait on Him. Prayer is not about lofty words offered to a distant God who expects perfection, it's merely honest words, a humble heart, and an expectation that God can do the miraculous. But even when your prayers aren't exactly selfless or humble, God still receives them and His grace covers impure motives.

You learn by doing, so just start!

7

Be Beautifully Authentic

*I*t is refreshing to talk with someone who is comfortable in her own skin, at ease, and willing to share struggles and imperfections as freely as joys and triumphs. Being rooted and grounded in Christ, you know who you are: a priceless daughter of the King, perfectly and wonderfully made in His image! This allows you to walk securely, letting others in on the real you. Your authenticity is a breath of fresh air in a stuffy world.

8

Develop Good Habits

*T*he woman you will be years from now is being formed by how you live today. Your habits set the stage for your future, so work to break the bad ones and replace them with better ones. The best habit to form is having regular time with the Lord. This habit can grow into a passion, and thankfully, when the passion wanes, the habit will keep you going. Other habits that are foundational in life are regular church attendance, maintaining an organized home, consistent exercise, and serving in the community. Intentionally develop your own good habits and many blessings will follow.

9

Seek God's Vision for Your Life

Living out God's vision for your life is thrilling! Start by surrendering your will to His and obeying Scripture. Pray. Ask God for His specific direction, then be attentive to the nudges you feel, using God's Word as your plumb line.

Think about your gifts and passions: how is God putting these to work in your life? He has wired you to thrive; living in sync with His vision will lead to abundant life!

10

Guard Your Heart

Your heart is precious and tender, full of ideas, dreams, and desires. In God's hands it is safe, protected by His loving care. Remembering you are a beloved daughter of the King and are of great worth will safeguard you from believing lies and living recklessly. God's Word says to guard your heart above all else because everything flows from it, all thoughts, words, and deeds.

*Seek first the kingdom of
God and his righteousness,
and all these things
will be added to you.*

MATHEW 6:33 ESV

11

Make the Most of Your Time

*S*trike a balance between scheduling and being spontaneous and you will make the most of your time. Thoughtful planning is important so think through your day or week; fill in your planner so you know what's coming and can take advantage of the open spaces. But be willing to throw plans and schedules out the window once in a while. Surprises pop up and will require switching gears. Jesus was both thoughtful and interruptible; you will learn to make the most of your time as you follow Him.

12

Offer and Accept Forgiveness

When you have hurt someone, humbly accept responsibility and ask for forgiveness. You may not feel like extending an olive branch, but do it anyway; it will keep bitterness from taking root. When someone has hurt you, graciously forgive them even if they don't ask for it. Forgiveness unlocks the door of your heart, welcoming in healing and freedom.

13

Journal Your Thoughts

Putting your thoughts and feelings on paper will help you reflect and become a thoughtful communicator. Journaling is also a great way to record your prayers. Your journals will become a treasure for your family. When future generations read them they will hear your heart and know your values. You will be leaving a lasting legacy.

14

Be a FAT Christian

Reading these words, you may think, "What the heck?" But as Anne Ortlund explained, the acronym FAT– Faithful, Available, and Teachable–is a brilliant way to remember what's most important. Being faithful, you will long to know Jesus and live life following His ways. Being available and taking time to prioritize your walk with the Lord, you will demonstrate a teachable spirit, one that is humble and eager to listen and do what He asks.

15

Serve Others

I love the definition of service as "love in work clothes." Service can be as simple as helping around the house or traveling to faraway places to love and care for people in need. Either way, service puts others above self, sacrificing for the good of someone else. God has grown your heart to serve as you've set the table, folded clothes, and cleaned up. You've learned to put others above yourself and respect those around you. These simple, everyday deeds have prepared you to love and serve well. Be attentive and God will surely put your training to good use for His kingdom purposes.

16

Extend True Friendship

Friendship is a gift you give and receive. A true friend is someone who loves and accepts you and makes a difference in your world. She is loyal, supportive, always has your back; she is honest even when it's hard and happily shares in your success. She brings out the best in you, and with her you are at ease. She is someone you love being with. Being a true friend makes an imprint on another heart that lasts a lifetime.

A friend loves at all times.

PROVERBS 17:17

*As iron sharpens iron, so one
person sharpens another.*

PROVERBS 27:17

17

Revel in the Art of God

Get outside and enjoy the beauty of nature. Wherever you are, take in your surroundings and notice the beautiful details: the colors, the smells, the creatures—all are God's handiwork. Nurturing your love of nature will help you to appreciate beauty in many aspects of life. Celebrate creation and praise the Creator!

18

Look Up

*M*ake certain places "no phone zones."
Church services, mealtimes, and date nights
are perfect times to keep your phone turned
off. Look up when you are in public. Give
others eye contact and share your smile.
Quickly you'll realize how silly people look
walking around glued to their phones.
Looking up frees you to notice what is going
on in the world around you, to be present
and engaged where you are.

19

Stay on Course

Growing to know God and walking in His ways can feel like a long and tiring journey. Choosing the right path will make all the difference. Half-hearted devotion, valuing the wrong opinions, justifying behavior, or focusing on outward appearance are tempting shortcuts but will never get you to your desired end point: heart transformation! Stay attentive and follow Jesus, and every once in a while take a look back; you'll be amazed how far you've come. When you stay the course, over time the journey will feel like an exciting faith adventure.

20

Practice Good Manners

Good manners express courtesy and will earn you respect. Keep your elbows off the table, don't interrupt while another is speaking, defer to your elders, and say "please" and "thank you." Elementary as they seem, you'd be surprised how often these simple rules are broken. Your good manners show you are aware of others and can be counted on to be polite in any situation. In no time at all good manners will be second nature.

Manners are a sensitive awareness of the feelings of others. If you have that awareness, you have good manners, no matter what fork you use.

EMILY POST

21

Love Sacrificially

True love is when you care more about meeting the other person's needs than having your own needs met. In a culture that promotes living for self, looking out for number one, "if you're not first, you're last," this seems almost scandalous. Loving another as God loves you means sacrifice and service. This isn't easy, especially as you face challenges and differences with the person you love. Keeping Jesus central in your relationships and relying on Him will strengthen you for the charge of truly loving another—in marriage and in other relationships. Loving sacrificially is possible because Jesus loved us first.

22

Learn from Wise People

Make it a priority to learn from those who are older and wiser than you. When you need help, look to an elder you trust who will listen, pray, and support you as you work through your issue. Often someone a little older can share from their experiences, offering hope, encouragement, and wisdom from God's Word.

23

Ask Interesting Questions

*B*e interested in others and you will become a great conversationalist. People love to talk about themselves so ask questions about family, interests, travel, favorites, etc. When you are genuinely interested in others it shows. Engage others and people will love talking with you.

24

Appreciate Beautiful You!

One of the most important and most difficult things to remember and try to practice is to be happy being you. The simple words "You'll never be the best so-and-so but you will always be the best YOU" is so true! At times you may question yourself, especially when you want to fit in or be accepted. But be brave and be you! Your heavenly Father knitted you together with wisdom, love, and care. You are just as He intended. If people love you for who you are, wonderful, good for them! If not, most likely they are not the kind of friend you want anyway. Trust me on this: You are beautiful just as you are.

*Your hands made me
and formed me; give me
understanding to learn
your commands. May those
who fear you rejoice when
they see me, for I have
put my hope in your word.*

PSALM 119:73–74 NIV

25

Hold On to Hope

Life is full of ups and downs. I like "up" days when I feel healthy and optimistic. But there will be days when you're staring at an impossible situation, seeing no way out. I wish those were few and far between, but there's no guarantee. On those days, hold onto hope and do what you know. Whisper a prayer: "Jesus, You are my rescue!" as many times as it takes to believe it. Open your Bible and digest truth until you feel satisfied. Sing the words to a beloved hymn until it becomes your declaration.

Seeking truth and choosing to believe it will challenge your will at first. In time, your heart will follow, clearing the way for renewed hope.

26

Practice Hospitality

Welcome friends, family, and strangers (like exchange students) into your home. Your warmth and generosity will nourish the souls of those on the receiving end of your hospitality. Keep in mind it is not about having a Pinterest-perfect home or being an excellent cook; a couple simple recipes and a willing heart is all you need. Making room at your table, saying "what is mine is yours" reflects the kindness of God, offering a little slice of heaven to all who walk through your door.

27

Give Thanks

*E*very day brings opportunities to give thanks to God. Good health, a family that adores you, sweet friends, a warm, cozy bed, loyal pals, your siblings, breath in your lungs—all are blessings you could easily take for granted. Focusing on all you have, not what you want, will help build contentment, even on a bad day. Giving thanks in the hard times may feel disingenuous at first, but keep at it and your thanks will become heartfelt. Persisting in thankfulness, you'll realize no matter what you are going through, God is with you. This will help keep life in perspective.

28

Pursue Simplicity

Living simply trains you to open your hands, loosening your grip on stuff, freeing you to offer what's yours to someone who really needs it. Simplicity is worth pursuing, but trust me, it's not easy when materialism tries to convince you your wants are really must-haves. Push back, cultivate gratitude, and in time you will learn to be happy with less. Simplicity makes room to appreciate and enjoy what you already have. That's contentment!

Be content with what you

have, because God has said,

"Never will I leave you;

never will I forsake you."

HEBREWS 13:5 NIV

29

Choose Your Words Wisely

Words are powerful; they can bless
and encourage or tear down and destroy.
I hope you will be an encourager. Use the
acronym THINK as a guide and you will never
have to eat humble pie. Ask yourself, is it true,
honorable, inspiring, necessary, kind?
If not, I suggest keeping it to yourself.
You'll grow wiser as you exercise
discipline with your words.

30

Send Handwritten Notes

*I*n our technological world of e-mail, text messages, and Twitter, a handwritten note is a special gift! E-mails in your inbox are a dime a dozen; a handwritten note in your mailbox is something to celebrate. Send notes to say "Thank you," "I love you," "I miss you," "Thinking of you," "Congratulations," or to share a simple observation. Your thoughtfulness will surprise and delight the recipient. Stock up on cards so you can send a note a week. In no time your paper trail of love and affection will be miles long.

31

Get to Know Yourself

With the barrage of Snapchat stories, Instagram posts, and Facebook feeds, many people seem to know other people better than they know themselves. Figuring out who you are requires thought and reflection, but understanding what you think and how you feel is worth the effort. Drown out the noise and turn off your phone so you can process what's happening IRL (in real life). Learn to ask yourself and others, "How do you feel?" Depth and authenticity make for an engaging, thoughtful person.

32

Give Generously

Giving generously blesses those on the receiving end of your gift and brings joy to the heart of the ultimate Giver. Your time, talent, and treasures are valuable gifts you can give away. Be creative and start small. Soon you'll understand how good it feels to be generous and you will become a cheerful giver. If you ever feel a bit like Scrooge, count your blessings and give anyway.

33

Pray for Our Troops

Take time to pray for the men and women in the military who serve our country and protect our freedom. They make tremendous sacrifices for our liberty and deserve our respect, support, and prayers. And don't forget the brave ones who've come home from battle. Many return with deep emotional and physical wounds, feeling lost or forgotten. Show you care and thank them for serving. Ask their names, remind them Jesus loves them, and commit to praying for them. Your words and kindness may offer renewed strength and faith at just the right time.

34

Trust God with Your Plans

Trust that the goals you hope to accomplish are in God's hands. He holds the keys to your future and will be faithful to direct your steps. By letting Him in on your plans, then being open to His will and trusting the outcome to His care, chances are great that you'll end up right where you should be. His plans may surprise or even scare you, but rest assured, if He calls you into something, He will provide what you need every step of the way.

*Trust in the Lord with all
your heart and lean not
on your own understanding;
in all your ways acknowledge
him, and he will make
your paths straight.*

PROVERBS 3:5–6 NIV

35

Be Available to Others

*I*n our fast-paced world it's easy to miss the lonely, hurting people among us. Being available to your friends shows them you care and will help you notice when something's just not right. Connect face-to-face when you can, otherwise pick up the phone and call. The smallest gesture can lead to a great reward. Just being there makes all the difference, and communicates, "You matter to me!"

36

Expect Struggles

Don't be surprised by difficult circumstances; God's Word tells us to expect them. Life is our training ground and no one makes it through without a few bumps and bruises. Consider these the battle scars that add character and depth to your story, making you relatable to others and useful to God. Challenges are often the very thing God uses to grow us the most. This is called sanctification.

37

Embrace Accountability

Accountability is protection that keeps you from getting stuck in a rut and encourages you to grow into the person God intends you to be. Being accountable to another person helps you stick to your commitments, knowing she will be following up. A friend willing to hold you accountable wants the best for you and will expect the best in you. Look for a friend who isn't afraid to ask hard questions, challenge behavior, and speak the truth in love, and you may have found a great accountability partner.

38

Ask for a "Do-Over"

Good communication requires time and practice. Once in a while you may ask yourself, *What just happened?* when feeling exasperated after a frustrating conversation. This is a good time to gather your courage and ask for a do-over, a chance to rewind and leave raised voices and defensiveness at the door, to humbly begin again. Put this into practice and you will refine your hard-earned communication skills. If you'll listen intently, ask questions to clarify, and respond with respect, you can offer comfort, which trumps "being right" or winning the fight. A do-over combined with prayer makes for a much happier ending.

39

Learn to Listen

A good listener makes you feel like you're the most important person in the room. They ask questions to clarify, not to form opinions or formulate a response. You know someone is truly interested when they listen intently. Feeling heard and understood opens the door for good, honest communication free from competition and drama. Listen to others as you would like them to listen to you.

40

Practice Discernment

*M*uch of what we see and hear in the world is immoral, so guard your heart and mind by choosing carefully what you allow to influence you. Protect yourself against things that will assault your senses or numb you to sin. You won't regret skipping the raunchy movie or saying no to the kids who just want an excuse to drink. Protecting yourself as a special, loved child of God is worth the effort.

This is my prayer:
that your love may abound
more and more in knowledge
and depth of insight,
so that you may be able
to discern what is best
and may be pure and
blameless for the day of Christ

PHILIPPIANS 1:9–10 NIV

41

Be a Role Model

No matter how old you are, there will always be younger girls who need your positive influence. Invest in them. Share your joys and struggles and you will be offering a beautiful gift of authenticity. You know girls feel pressure to measure up to an unrealistic standard, often getting caught in the rat race of competition and comparison. Hearing from you and learning there is a better way, allows them to breathe a sigh of relief.

42

Let Your Light Shine

The light of Christ lives within you, and on any given day your simple interactions with others will point to Jesus. As you reflect God's goodness, grace, and love, the world will notice there's something different about you and want what you have. Let your light shine bright, unhindered by the opinions of others, and you will have an open door to share the hope that you have!

43

Celebrate
Imperfection

You've grown up in a day when social media highlights perfection in every arena of life, leaving many feeling "less-than." Understand these photos flaunting flawless people—weddings, crafts, dorm rooms, homes—aren't reality. Besides, who wants the stress and pressure of living up to a crazy standard of perfection? One look at the magazine rack at the market tells you perfection is not all it's cracked up to be. Imperfections are endearing; they help others relax and feel free to be themselves. So put away any notions of being perfect and embrace imperfections in yourself and others.

44

Seek Respect Not Popularity

Remember, it's great to be well liked,
it's important to be well respected,
but being popular is overrated. People
are often popular for the wrong reasons.
Be your kind, sincere self and people will
be drawn to you for the right reasons.

45

Read the Bible Cover to Cover

Commit to reading the Bible from Genesis to Revelation at least once. You will learn fascinating truths about courageous people who walked faithfully with the Lord and discover books you didn't even know existed. Reading from start to finish, you will develop a greater understanding of the big God story, of which you are a part. And the best news: God speaks through His Word, imparting truth page by page.

46

Learn to Say No

Learning to say no takes practice,
but it is worth the effort. You can't possibly
do everything asked of you all the time,
that would leave you running on empty.
Consider the request; if you feel it's a no,
reply honestly without letting guilt get the
best of you. Your no makes a way for another
person's yes and leaves you free to pursue
the things you're called to.

*Beware the barrenness
of a busy life.*

SOCRATES

*A women who lives with
the stress of an overwhelmed
schedule will often ache
with the sadness of an
underwhelmed soul.*

LYSA TERKURST

47

Step Outside Your Comfort Zone

Try new things that challenge you and offer opportunities for growth. Being open to new experiences will keep life interesting and prevent you from stagnating. A little change now and then is good. You never know what fascinating people you might discover, or what passion may be hiding along the way.

48

Listen to the People Who Love You

*Y*ou know who your people are: the tribe that shares your name as well as friends you rely on to be there to care for your heart. They're the ones you'll struggle with, but they'll also have your back when you go to battle. When you are too close to a situation—or to yourself!—they can offer valuable perspective. If you venture near a slippery slope, they will be the truth tellers who risk offending you rather than watching you slide down that hill. They have fought with you but also fought for you, so they've earned the right to be heard. Be humble and listen to them!

49

Be on Time

*B*eing timely shows others you value them. It says, "I know your time is important; I will not make you wait on me." Situations arise that are beyond your control, but as a rule, be on time. You will be known as someone who is dependable and respectful of others.

50

De-Clutter

De-clutter your room by getting rid of unnecessary stuff that simply collects dust. De-clutter your closet by giving away some of the T-shirts you've collected from teams, camps, and vacations. De-clutter your social accounts by saying *adios* to people you don't know personally or don't want seeing your personal posts. Getting rid of the mess and excess makes way for order and ushers in a sense of calm and freedom.

51

Keep Your Doors Open

Keep your front door wide open so you can welcome in new opportunities of growth and service. Then, let the less important things out the back door. This principle will help you make wise choices about how to spend your time. Be prayerful before saying yes, as letting too many things in the front door without ushering a few things out the back will leave you feeling overwhelmed. Having the front and back doors open has helped me manage time and commitments, saving me from the craziness of an overcommitted life.

52

Beware of Pride

*B*eware of foolish pride. It is ugly, damaging, and sneaky. It hides behind many masks: subtle self-promotion, false humility, unhealthy competition, need for attention, compliment fishing. Pride is an airbrushed selfie. Anytime you're convinced someone else is your problem, you can be sure pride has gotten the best of you. The good news: humility defuses pride. Seek Jesus and you'll see humility is kind and inclusive, expressing "all are welcome here." Humility doesn't clamor for attention or need to be center stage; it defers to others willingly. Lay down your pride and any notion that it's all about you. In time, God will replace your self-importance with a gentle spirit of humility, a far greater reward.

53

Look for a True Gentleman

*Y*ou know what a gentleman looks like; you've observed for years. Men of character who practice "ladies first"—opening your door, being an attentive listener, and using respectful language—are great to watch for. But keep in mind not every young man has had a great role model, so don't expect perfection. Always remember you are worthy of a gentleman, but if he has a kind heart and a teachable spirit and a noble love for God, he'll become a gentleman in training. Your nonnegotiables, support, and grace will encourage him to become the man God intends.

54

Return Your Shopping Cart

I have seen many runaway carts bang into unsuspecting cars when someone thought it was another's job to return it. Returning the cart doesn't take long and shows courtesy and respect for others. With a little effort this simple gesture will soon become a habit. And caring for others in the small things ensures you're paying attention when the big things come up.

55

Start Each Day in Prayer

"Good morning, Lord! This is Your day, I am Your child, show me Your way!" This is my petition most mornings before my feet hit the floor. I turn the reins over to God, knowing the details of my life are best left with Him. As I start each day asking for guidance, He is faithful to direct and redirect when I get in the way. Recognize God's presence early and pay attention to the promptings of the Holy Spirit throughout each day. Jesus is with you ready to guide as you stay attentive.

Teach me your way,
O Lord, and I will walk
in your truth; give me
an undivided heart
that I may fear your name.

PSALM 86:11 NIV

56

Lend a Helping Hand

The world is full of hurting, needy people. You don't have to look far to see someone who could use your help. Ask the Lord to guide you as you see people in need. And if you aren't sure what to do, pray! Your heartfelt prayers will bless the homeless man on the corner or the people who've just been in a car accident. If you let the Holy Spirit be your guide, you will notice the needs around you and can partner with God to bless His people.

57

Keep the Cookie Jar Full

Find a recipe you love and make it over and over. Your family will love having homemade treats on hand and their friends will know they can count on something yummy when they come to your home. And if you need to bring a gift somewhere but don't have much money, you can always bake!

58

Use Soul Words

There is great wisdom in learning to use descriptive "soul words" when sharing your feelings. Replace nondescript words like fine or frustrated with expressive soul words that convey your feelings, and you will unlock a deeper level of communication, fostering intimacy in your family and friends. Words like elated, jolted, distressed, comforted, provoked, or detached take the guesswork out of communication. You can download a list at howwelove.com/resources. Keep it handy. And don't be afraid to ask others to use it to nurture their emotional health and meaningful connection too.

59

Tithe

Develop the habit of tithing early. Start with 10 percent and grow from there. Your home church, missionaries, sponsored Compassion kids, or local ministries are all worthy of your resources. You will be blessed seeing how God uses your gifts, and want to give more.

60

Share Your Story

Take opportunities to share your story. Think of it as testifying to the work God is doing in your life and it won't seem hard or scary. Sharing your victories will inspire others to remain faithful, and the failures you sense may disqualify you will keep you relatable and useful to God. Your story is a powerful tool that can capture the attention of others, open them up to their own growth, and point to the goodness of our God.

61

Develop Family Traditions

Traditions are unifying and so much fun! They nurture a sense of belonging and bond a family together. Traditions can be serious, silly, or somewhere in between. Affirmations and a special banner on birthdays, Christmas caroling with family and friends, building resurrection tombs at Easter, a fun family cheer, or a formal blessing ceremony at a milestone birthday will become anticipated rituals that make your family uniquely YOU! Set your family traditions in stone and look forward to building cherished memories for years to come.

I have come that they

may have life,

and have it to the full.

JOHN 10:10 NIV

62

Apologize in Person

When you have hurt someone and need to apologize, whenever possible, do it in person. Accepting responsibility for your actions isn't easy, but it is the right thing to do. When you are sincerely sorry, the other person will see it in your eyes and feel it as you humble yourself. Moving forward will be easier because you have made amends in person.

63

Take a Rest

God values rest! In fact, it is one of His ten commandments. Don't dismiss this command; it's there for good reason. Learning to balance work and rest will protect you from a breathless pace and constant striving. Begin to take a regular Sabbath from all work, social media, projects, etc. Make it your goal to make no progress at all for one day in order to rest, renew, and rejuvenate. This work-rest rhythm takes practice, but once in place, it will breathe peace and hope into your tired, weary soul.

64

Remember You're a Masterpiece

How amazing it is to be uniquely created by God! You are His masterpiece, perfectly and wonderfully made in His image! You are a priceless daughter of the King, loved unconditionally. Your heavenly Father takes great delight in you. Speak these words until the truth is settled in your heart. Then live confidently in the reality of who you are!

I have loved you with
an everlasting love;
I have drawn you
with unfailing kindness.

JEREMIAH 31:3 NIV

65

Nurture Your Sense of Adventure

Continue to pursue adventure and you will have some wonderful experiences. You will never forget the thrill of diving deep into a mountain lake or discovering a new talent to pursue. An adventurous spirit requires courage, but each time you conquer a fear you'll gain confidence, making the next adventure a little less scary.

66

Be a Good Citizen of Heaven & Earth

Your true citizenship is in heaven; your eternal future is secured. But God has planted you here for now and you have a part to play. Remember freedom is a privilege; voting is a responsibility. Do your part! When considering candidates for public office, take time to learn what each person stands for. Look for someone who represents your values and whose track record shows they are willing to fight for what is most important to you. But keep in mind no leader is perfect and no country is flawless. Your true hope is in Jesus and your real home is heaven!

67

Give Yourself
a Break

Life is full of schedules, routines, and obligations. When you need a break from the crazy pace and pressures, allow yourself the freedom to hit pause. Call a friend, say a prayer, or take a walk and get some fresh air. Sometimes a short diversion is all you'll need to feel refreshed and rejuvenated.

68

Dress Up Now and Again

Looking good and feeling good are connected. Don't discount that. God made you to appreciate beauty and spread it by your very presence. So dress up once in a while. Jeans are fine for most days, but every now and again, even if you are just going to the market or out to lunch, give the jeans a break and put on something feminine. And make sure you have a versatile black dress. This one article of clothing will be worth paying a little extra for, you will have many opportunities to wear it, and a nice black dress is always in style.

69

Pursue Good Health

Keeping active and eating right will help you enjoy good health. Eating right is a personal commitment, but know that your heart and body are connected. Follow what your heart needs and what your body needs and you won't be tempted to use food to fix emotional struggles. Pay attention to how you respond to different foods, and as a general rule, eat natural: leafy greens, nuts, and berries are always good, but limit processed foods and refined sugar. Listen to how you feel, make choices accordingly, and you will be promoting good health.

70

Commit the Bible to Memory

Commit time to memorizing Scripture, and God's Word will be with you no matter where you are. When you are tossed by life's waves, memorized passages are an anchor, reminding you you're secure. You will know how to find life "to the full" (John 10:10) and find rest for your soul, for His "burden is light" (Matthew 11:30). When the Word is hidden in your heart, the beauty of a sunset can cause Scripture to spontaneously bubble out in praise! God's voice over all others will drown out the noise—and that is good news!

For out of the overflow of the heart the mouth speaks.

MATTHEW 12:34 NIV

Your Word is a lamp to my feet and a light to my path.

PSALM 119:105 NIV

71

Go to Church, Be the Church

Church is where we go *and* who we are. When
you find one that teaches the Bible, reaches
out beyond its walls to share the love and hope
of Jesus, and welcomes you with open arms,
get plugged in! You have a role to play and
if you are willing, God will put your gifts
and passion to good use for you and for
the benefit of others. Your church community
will become your extended family as you
link arms and live out the gospel together.

72

Work Hard, Play Hard

Learning to balance work and play requires skill. A strong work ethic can protect you from laziness and entitlement, and fighting for downtime to play will keep you from becoming a workaholic. Both are important. Putting boundaries around work and having someone to hold you accountable helps. Keep in mind balance is the goal, but don't beat yourself up if you don't do this perfectly. It takes time, but working hard and making sure there is time for play is worth it!

73

Pray for Patience

When life is frustrating or people are annoying, pray for patience. Every day offers opportunities to grow in patience; leaning in and asking God for help is important. Patient people are loving people; they aren't easily rattled and seem to take things in stride. Patience also comes in handy when you have to wait for things you want, like an answer to a question, a package in the mail, or a much-needed change. I've heard it said, "Patience is bitter but its fruit is sweet!"

74

Live to the Glory of God

Living life to God's glory means pleasing Him above all else. You will bring God glory in large and small ways as you journey from day to day. Choosing deeper joy when feeling discouraged over a frustrating situation brings God glory. Refusing to engage in gossip brings Him glory. Standing firm in truth when it would be easy to turn a blind eye brings Him glory. Obedience and submission to God's will brings Him glory. Every day is a blank slate of opportunities to honor God and live for His glory.

75

Be Brave

You are a courageous young woman and I've seen you stand up for the things you know are right. You have faced challenges that would compromise your values, yet you have weathered each storm steadfast in your convictions. Compromising your values will leave you sad and empty; following God's plan brings freedom and abundant life. I hope you always choose life!

76

Play Games

Playing games is a great, inexpensive way to spend an evening. Game night brings people together and gives everyone a chance to let loose and have fun. Monopoly, Rummikub, and Taboo are all family favorites that require creativity, strategy, and a sense of humor. So gather a group, pull out the games, and watch the dynamics unfold. If you want to make sure your game night is lively, invite at least a couple competitive types; they keep things exciting!

77

Eliminate and Concentrate

Eliminate the things in life that don't count for eternity and concentrate on the things that do. Anne Ortlund used to say, "If you live for something other than Jesus you will end up soft, unfulfilled, and mediocre. And who wants that?" Don't allow what you value most to be crowded out by less important things. As you invest your time in furthering God's kingdom, you will be making a difference for all eternity.

78

Have a Weekly Meeting

Take time each week to meet individually with each member of your family. The goal is to have a regular time to check-in and share a few important details. Keeping it simple and positive will make it something everyone will look forward to. Here are some questions to get you started:

What's God been teaching you this week? What was the greatest joy of the week? The greatest struggle of the week? Share an affirmation, a wish, or a hope. Review each other's calendar. Ask how you can pray for them. Close in prayer.

79

Learn to Respond, Not React

Responding is saying something in reply to another; reacting means you are responding with emotion. See the difference? Bite your tongue if it will keep you from blurting out something you may regret, and practice responding with care instead. Learning how to respond eliminates drama and helps you communicate thoughtfully. Learning this earlier in life would have helped me avoid a lot of unnecessary arguments. I hope you will learn and practice now.

*A gentle answer
turns away wrath,
but a harsh word
stirs up anger.*

PROVERBS 15:1 NIV

*From the mouth
of the righteous comes
the fruit of wisdom.*

PROVERBS 10:31 NIV

80

Submit to a Higher Authority

As a Christian you must obey the law, but ultimately you submit to a higher authority. There is pressure to compromise in many areas of life. Underage drinking, texting while driving, disregarding speed limits, sex before marriage, are all issues that could be dismissed as silly rules you don't need to follow. Know you can hold yourself to a higher standard, look to God's Word as your authority, and trust that His precepts lead to life as He intended.

81

Make Home Your Happy Place

Being busy at home fosters a love for all the happenings within its walls. Whether you are at work or home, temptations to be busy elsewhere will be plentiful. Focusing your attention on home will make room for simple things that bond a family together: family dinners, sharing burdens, praying together, important conversations, timely hugs, and so much more. Making home your happy place is foundational in nurturing a close-knit family!

82

Recognize the Pain of Sin

Like thunder and lightning, sin and pain always go together. When we violate God's standard, consequences follow. These consequences might be hard and painful but they are for our good, keeping us from further sin and separation from God. Consequences are often the very thing God uses to grow us into maturity.

83

Grace Follows Repentance

We know nothing can separate us from the love of God. But sin leaves us feeling guilty and unworthy. The enemy desires we stay trapped in sin, because he knows that while we are stuck he has a hold on us. When we confess and repent, our sin is exposed and it no longer has power over us. Repentance opens the door to receive the gift of God's amazing, lavish grace.

84

Write and Memorize Your Simple Prayer

$\mathcal{A}$ short prayer expressing your desire to be attentive to God's work around you, placed in strategic spots around the house, can remind you what's most important. Inscribed on your heart, a simple prayer will continue to be your hope. It can be something like: "Lord, open my eyes that I might see You. Open my ears that I may hear You. Open my heart that I would understand all that You have for me today." I encourage you to write your own prayer or memorize another that expresses your desire for growth. God will be faithful to answer as you pray.

85

Dream Big, Pray Big

Have fun pursuing your dreams, praying boldly for God's blessing. If your dream is not in line with His, He will let you know. Look for open doors and pay attention to closed doors; these may be the Lord's yes or no. If your dream does not align with God's will, let it go. This may be hard, but releasing it could be the key to unlocking a richer, more fulfilling dream you didn't even know was in you.

86
Set Goals

*I*f you want to live purposefully, setting goals is a worthy practice. Think and pray about what you'd like to accomplish or how you hope to grow, and set a few measurable, realistic goals. Sharing your goals with a trusted friend or mentor who will encourage and hold you accountable will help. Start with six-month goals and reassess after three months. It is gratifying to set and achieve the goals you've set.

87

Accept Embarrassing Moments

$\mathcal{E}$veryone experiences embarrassment at some point. It might be as harmless as calling someone the wrong name or tripping on a rug. Or it could be more awkward, like asking someone when their baby is due only to hear them reply, "I had her three weeks ago." There are worse things in life than being embarrassed. No matter what is said or done, do your best to graciously move on. You don't need to make excuses or talk your way out of it; it is a perfect time to apply the rule *less is more*.

88

Wisdom Takes Time

We all want to be wise and discerning, able to manage the challenging situations that arise in life, but it can be frustrating to feel like it's one step forward, two steps back. Growing in wisdom requires patience; laying a sturdy foundation that will hold when the storms of life rage comes through daily choices, brick by brick. Don't allow mistakes to derail you; a person becomes wise by learning from what happens when she wasn't. That's the best news: God will never stop working to accomplish the good work started in you!

89

Continually Reassess

What we really believe is shown in our actions.
These words, paraphrased from the Bible
(1 John 3:18), have served as a reality check for me.
We can say we believe in this or that, but how
we spend our time really exposes what we value.
I can convince you loving God and following His ways
is my first priority, but if I spend all my time doing
other things, there's been a disconnect.
I haven't always made the right choices, and what
I say I value and how I spend my time don't always
line up. Acknowledging this, I hope you too will
ask God for the courage to continually reassess
and live according to His priorities for your life.

90

Pass It On

A mentor can leave an enduring mark on your life. When you love the Lord and His Word, you'll want to share with others. Make discipleship your passion. Passing on truth that has changed your life and watching others grow in faith is a beautiful privilege. As you grow, look for an older, wiser, faithful woman to take you under her wing and learn from her. As you mature, share what you've learned with younger women; they will grow following your example. Discipleship is a wonderful calling and produces beautiful fruit!

*Therefore go and make
disciples of all nations,
baptizing them in the name
of the Father and of the Son
and of the Holy Spirit,
and teaching them to
obey everything I have
commanded you. And surely
I am with you always,
to the very end of the age.*

MATTHEW 28:19–20 NIV

91

Have Open Arms

*I*t is important to attend church regularly, but it is essential to be the church outside its walls. Putting God's Word into practice and loving your neighbor puts the gospel on display for those who may never step inside a church building. When you put your agenda on hold to help someone in need, extend grace instead of hold a grudge, show love to someone who is hard to love, you are being a doer of the word and loving your neighbor.

92

Talk Like a Lady

It is always attractive when a lady chooses not to swear or use inappropriate slang. Value yourself and others enough to use respectable language. People will notice and appreciate you for it.

93

Get to Know the Neighbors

When new neighbors move in, introduce yourself and offer a warm welcome. Nothing says "We're glad you're here" like being offered warm cookies fresh from the oven. Give them your contact information in case of emergency. A list of names of everyone on your street can be very helpful too. These are simple gestures but will make a big impact, opening the door for future conversation and real friendship.

94

Do Not Conform

Don't be like the proverbial frog in water, so immersed in culture you can't tell you're being scalded to death. Romans 12:2 urges: "Do not conform to the pattern of this world, but be transformed" (NIV). A transformed heart stands firm under pressure even when it feels like it's standing alone. It influences culture for good, putting the gospel on display wherever it's planted. And the gospel—God's love for all—is the hope of the world!

Since you have heard about Jesus and have learned the truth that comes from him, throw off your old sinful nature and your former way of life, which is corrupted by lust and deception. Instead, let the Spirit renew your thoughts and attitudes. Put on your new nature, created to be like God— truly righteous and holy.

EPHESIANS 4:21–24 NLT

95

Choose to Be Honorable

Your reputation is what others think of you; character is what God knows to be true. Daily choices are the training ground for character development. How you treat the barista, what you do with the twenty-dollar bill the girl walking by dropped, or how you handle the chance to cheat, all expose your character. How you respond when no one is looking is a great barometer of who you are. Excellent character will earn you a great reputation, and that is priceless!

96

Be Dependable

Dependable doesn't sound exciting, but it's synonymous with trustworthy, loyal, faithful, and steadfast, all admirable qualities. When people know they can rely on you to do what you've said, they relax knowing you won't let them down. Being dependable means you are someone who can be counted on. And who doesn't want a friend like that?

97

Be Present

Cameras used to be reserved for special occasions. Photos of your dinner, outfit, or facial expressions wasn't the thing it is now. You can love photos and memorializing important events, but remember life is more than capturing the perfect photo. Be present wherever you are; enjoy those you are with and what you're doing. Live life and don't spend time worrying about how many people "like" it.

98

Accept Difficult People

There is no way around it, sometimes people will annoy you and sometimes you will annoy others. We all have our quirks and no one is immune from a little dysfunction. As a rule, bear with your friends when they get on your nerves, realizing they most likely bear with you. When faced with more challenging situations, look to Philippians 4:8. If you can't "think about such things" up close with a friend, take a few steps back. Give God time and space to work. He will show you how to love and move forward with this person.

99

Don't Be a Lone Ranger

*W*hat's sharable is bearable. This is wisdom you'll learn, and hopefully not from years of stuffing feelings and pretending things were okay when they weren't. Being alone in your struggles can feel overwhelming and scary. But sharing will lighten your load and ease your burden. A fresh set of eyes and a different perspective might be all you need to feel better.

"Share your joy and it is doubled: share your burden and it is cut in half," has been true for me.

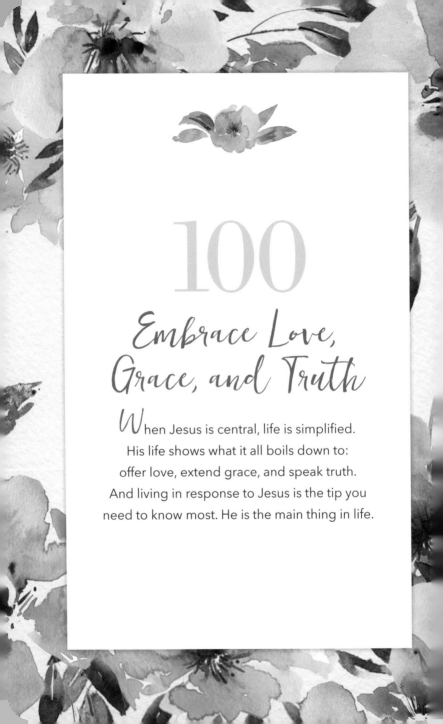

100

Embrace Love, Grace, and Truth

When Jesus is central, life is simplified.
His life shows what it all boils down to:
offer love, extend grace, and speak truth.
And living in response to Jesus is the tip you
need to know most. He is the main thing in life.

About the Author

Lisa Grable is a member of Compel, Proverbs 31 Ministries online writing community. Through years of Bible Study Fellowship her love for God's Word grew. While sitting at Anne Ortlund's table she cultivated a desire to pass on the truth that was changing her life. Lisa is a wife, mother, and ministry leader who is passionate about her family, discipleship, and encouraging women to fix their eyes on Jesus. She and her husband, Dan, share an empty nest in Newport Beach, California, and have three adult children.

$\mathcal{S}$ing, O Daughter of Zion...
Be glad and rejoice with all your heart....
The Lord your God is with you,
he is mighty to save.
He will take great delight in you,
he will quiet you with his love,
he will rejoice over you with singing.

ZEPHANIAH 3:14, 17 NIV84